A miscellany of devastating insults and sm
and funny oddities . . .

. . . things I wish I'd said at the time.

For people who get into arguments, write sp   . ...ɔ ᴎᴋᴇ to
play with language.

Culled over ten years mostly from comments on YouTube.

Table of Contents

ISBN: 9798584003920

www.seviourbooks.com

Disclaimer: Apart from a few exceptions, I am not the author of these remarks and I have no record of who is. But if you are and you'd like to be credited, please let me know.
ravelston@seviourbooks.com

Insults

To explain 'stupid' to aliens,
we could begin by describing you.

I promise I'll act like I care,
even though I really don't.

When he enters a room, his ego gets
there 10 feet before him.

I don't want to say 'bitchy' because
that would describe her perfectly.

If you are not too busy condescending me.

You aren't pretty, neither am I;
on that we are even.

I don't give a wet handkerchief.

Yours is the view from the window of a rocket that
has long slipped the surly bonds of reality.

Being fat drunk and stupid is no way
to go through life, son . . .

. . . Being a donkey is no way
to go through life either, dad.

That's right, you're wrong.

I'm looking forward to not knowing you.

Absolute dog waste: I reached for a plastic bag
after I read your remark.

Your day has passed, see you at the cemetery.

I thought of you today,
then I remembered to take out the trash.

You're trying so hard to be convincing that
[XXX] has been a banquet, when really,
it's a pile of rotting garbage.

Winters coming for you and your lot.

Your insincere and putrid remark
deserves no response.

You're trying to communicate,
I can tell, bless your heart.

You forgot to list being a moron
in your resume.

When he speaks, inert gas fills the room.

A little cheese with your whine?

Go flip hamburgers.

What a Giuliani you have become!

There's a 4-letter word beginning
with C to describe her. . . .
. . . . COLD.

You're welcome. . . .
. . . about as welcome as a
dose of clap in a nunnery.

Waiting for the day when you don't wake up.

Freeform rambling, noise devoid of all meaning.

He immatures with age.

Perhaps you should engage your brain
before your fingers.

Do you know who finds you
absolutely fascinating?

. . .You.

Pull your dress down little man,
your dumbfuckery is showing.

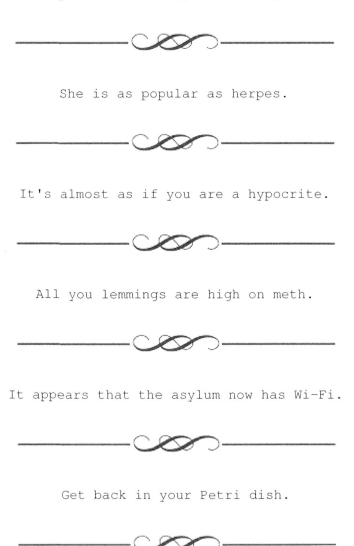

She is as popular as herpes.

It's almost as if you are a hypocrite.

All you lemmings are high on meth.

It appears that the asylum now has Wi-Fi.

Get back in your Petri dish.

Humour not your strong point I'm guessing? I bet
you're fun at parties.

I suspect you're just indulging in a bit of self-
pleasuring with that remark.

That aged well

Since you are resorting to personal attacks and not
actually trying to defend your original argument or
add anything else to your argument. I'm going to end
this now.

Jabroni, a loser, poser, lame-ass.

I'm not sure who to believe: On the one hand there are psychologists and behavioural therapists with solid evidence gained from scientific studies… On the other hand there is you and your assertions.

Based on the new information you've provided, I'd happily amend the above point to say '...you, your assertions and anecdotal evidence'.

Don't let a little knowledge get in the way of your prejudices.

My cats litter box is filled with things smarter than that piece of shit. Of course, with that I'm insulting things in the litter box.

She's a real C U Next Tuesday

— Harry Enfield

You are a funny fuck.

I laughed until I stopped.

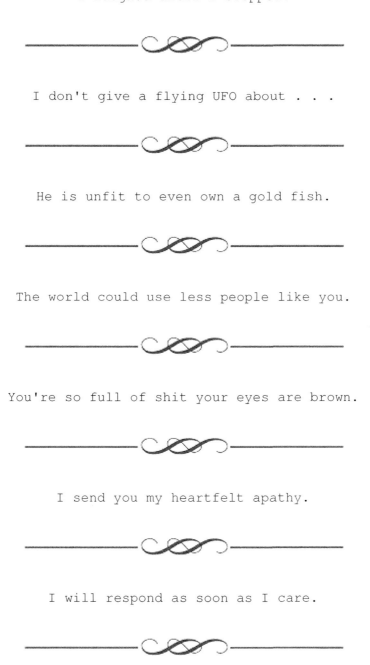

I don't give a flying UFO about . . .

He is unfit to even own a gold fish.

The world could use less people like you.

You're so full of shit your eyes are brown.

I send you my heartfelt apathy.

I will respond as soon as I care.

No one's perfect, especially you.

Change the record, it's as warped as your brain.

She's a beast in human garbage.

It's almost as if you're an unscrupulous opportunist
who blows whichever way
the wind goes.

He tripped and bruised his ego.

Couldn't happen to a nicer piece of shit.

A Poundland Paxman.

Wake me up before you gogo.

Please, say something half intelligent.

A spoon full of Clorox helps
the medicine go down - try some.

Your sewer-level character.

I'm busy right now, I'll ignore you later.

I am not insulting you; I am describing you.

If there is an infinite number of parallel universes, there may be one where you are popular.

I really feel for you when you talk about things you don't understand.

You're the reason that no one likes you.

We regret the vacancy has now been filled. Suggestion: try MacDonalds.

45 - of, and pertaining to

It was miraculous. It was almost no trick at all, to turn vice into virtue, slander into truth, impotence into abstinence, arrogance into humility, plunder into philanthropy, thievery into honor, blasphemy into wisdom, brutality into patriotism, and sadism into justice. Anybody could do it. It merely required no character.

Many believe Trump would not be president without the right-wing media ecosystem Murdoch created.

We'll see what happens

You sir, are a genius, and I say that very strongly.

(Thank you for) this / your powerful display of stable genius / for your profound ignorance.

His entire company is upside down,
bleeding red ink.

A man of no fixed beliefs other than in his own
right to rule

The 'billionaire who hides his tax returns. 'The
genius' who hides his college grades. The
'businessman' who bankrupted 3 casinos and lost
over $1B in 10 years. The 'playboy' who pays for
sex. The 'Christian' who doesn't go to church.
The 'philanthropist' who defrauds charity.
The 'patriot' who dodged the draft and attacks
dead Veterans and their widows.

The difference between a bean and a chickpea? Putin
doesn't have a tape of Trump
watching a bean.

Best words, pay off, tax return, toilet paper, handcuff, jail date, glass water, steep ramp, nobody knows, strong covefe.

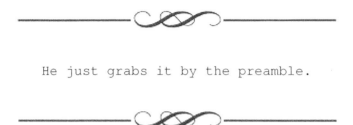

He just grabs it by the preamble.

There has been one disastrous mishap after another: quitting the Paris Agreement, quitting the Iran Deal, moving the US embassy to Jerusalem prompting a massacre, and now this North Korea failure. Trump should just concentrate on fucking up America.

Trump's qualifications do not extend beyond the ability to unwrap a cheeseburger.

Person, Man, Sucker, Loser, Trump.

His conscience is clean - it's never been used.

Handcuffs, jumpsuit, prison, solitary.

What the hell does he think war is, skipping through
a field of daisies singing Kumbaya?

Who lies more, rugs on the floor or DJT?

In the wasteland, only cockroaches and Mitch
McConnell may survive.

A sociopath who has the attention of a goldfish.

Trump has the IQ of a plastic spoon.

It's not over until the fat president sings.

If you thought that placing an unstable incompetent clown from reality TV into world's most important leadership position would be good for you, you are stupid. Not just plain stupid, but a special type of stupid; hupid. That's hate + stupid.

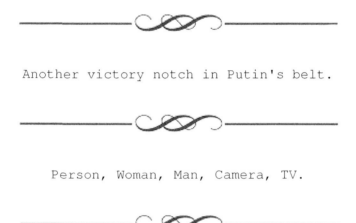

Another victory notch in Putin's belt.

Person, Woman, Man, Camera, TV.

The Don is a Lizard. Put him in a large tank and feed him Locusts and on Sundays Cockroaches.

The principal difference between Bannon and Trump is perfume. Both need to be bagged for curbside pickup.

I'm like a smart person. I know the biggest words, believe me. I'm a very stable genius?

A racist bigot in an obese shell – a Hero to the idiots who believed his rhetoric.

An unhinged proto-fascist.

When my Dad started acting like Trump
does we took the TV remote away from him,
we didn't give him a country to play with!

With each day, however, it's clearer that the secret
of Trump's success ischeating. He, and those around
him, don't have to be better than their opponents
because they're willing to be so much worse.

Trump does a brilliant impression of Alex Baldwin.

Trump is the blueprint for idiots and his
appallingly ignorant supporters are the finished
products.

Their revoltingly ostentatious Manhattan penthouse,
which is decorated in a style best described as
Dictator Chic.

A quintessential conman.

Every time he does that,
another angel loses its wings.

As we now know, being described in superlatives by
Trump almost always marks the subject
as an incompetent.

Nambia is such a bigly friend of the US.
We buy a lot of Covfefe from them.

Donald Trump: an ungodly amalgam of
Juan and Evita Peron.

Trump hasn't touched a drop of alcohol or mind
alerting drugs in his life.

Don't cry for Trump, America. The truth is, he'll never cry for you.

Melania: the gold digger's gold digger.

The first one-term president in years and the only one to lose the popular vote twice.

He will be remembered for what he was: a lying, racist, sexist, misogynist, colluding slug.

He's not lying, he's simply expressing sentiments he knows to be false.

I think I am actually humble. I think I'm much more humble than you would understand.

Marla Maples – 'Nice tits, no brains',
as he would later sum her up.

'His lack of education is more than compensated for
by his keenly developed moral bankruptcy.'

– Woody Allen

Impeached is forever.

Chlorox will erasethe evidence.

Do you know how bad you have to be for Paris to ring
church bells when you lose?
And fireworks in London?

We will ALWAYS worship him no matter what
THEY say about facts, or what he does wrong or
his silly lies. We don't care that he's a
narcissisticsociopath, serial liar, adulterer, draft
dodger, hates our POW soldiers, trusts the Russian
government over our own, discredits our brave FBI
officers, or that he's obviously
not sharpest tool in the shed...
he's OUR President.

It's the 'Gruesome Trainwreck' factor, but with an
orange haired petulant racist asshole instead of a
train.

Funnily Enough

Bees visit flowers. If they didn't you'd have nothing to eat. (Justifying men having affairs).

I took an online IQ test, and scoring 130,
it told me I am in the top two per cent.
'So did I' says Lauren.
Her friend tells her later,
'My dog could score 130 on that test'.

The wheels are coming off the/your submarine.

Who among us hasn't made that mistake . . .
. . . yesterday?

Like Vincent Van Gogh, I will never live to know how much my work will be loved and admired by future generations.

A grey moribund carbuncle on the arse-end of
Scotland. (Originally referring to the town of
Forth, South Lanarkshire, Scotland. There were many
contenders for this title. Google it.)

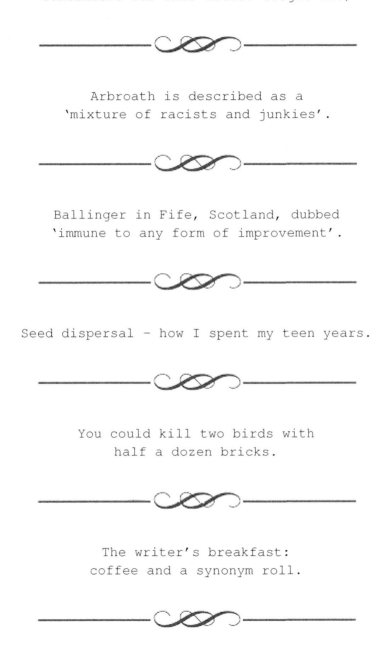

Arbroath is described as a
'mixture of racists and junkies'.

Ballinger in Fife, Scotland, dubbed
'immune to any form of improvement'.

Seed dispersal - how I spent my teen years.

You could kill two birds with
half a dozen bricks.

The writer's breakfast:
coffee and a synonym roll.

It's like an ocean with lots of water.

The rest is hysterics.

How come fire sauce isn't made with real fire?

(XXX) will be revealed in all its ignomy.

To know me is to love me.

First, . . .(this) . Now . . . (that),
I want a new planet!

Everything I write and say is true, be quiet.

That's just what they want you to believe!

I can confirm that 100% of wind turbine accidents
occur because of wind turbines.

It is still true what Voltaire said so long ago . .
. . . but did Voltaire ever envisage
a deep-fried Mars Bar?

'Foolish', you calling me 'foolish'?

Have you ever noticed how, when all the trees get
together and wiggle their limbs, it gets windy?

A land with no graveyards
is a country of cannibals.

Not knowing what Armageddon means
is not the end of the world.

Pubs are very educational,
full of experts on any
subject you like.

The early bird might get the worm,
but the second mouse gets the cheese.

His baroque private life.

You'll never be as lazy as
whoever named the fireplace.

I don't care if I'm a moron;
at least I'm a moron with standards.

My ignorance is as valid as your knowledge.

It's a dog eat dog world, and I will eat your dog.

Everyone laughed when I told them I wanted to be a comedian; well they're not laughing now.

The difference between ignorance and apathy?
I don't know and I don't care.

Dogs can analyse trajectories to intercept flying objects, but they're crap at explaining physics.

What's the use of happiness?
It can't buy you money.'

- Henny Youngman

Grammar - The difference between
knowing your sh!t
and
knowing you're sh!t.

Bees - the natural enemy of a tightrope walker.

I resemble your implication.

A man goes to the doctor with hearing problems.
'Can you describe the symptoms to me?'
'Yes. Homer is a fat yellow lazy bastard and
Marge is a skinny bird with big blue hair'

Don't blame me for your lack of incompetence.

I mean it with all the confidence
born of ignorance.

In *italics*, cause he's Italian.

I have two bad habits — smoking and masturbation.
I'm a thirty a day man and I smoke like a chimney.

German children are kinder.

Free violin, no strings attached.

'A nickel ain't worth a dime anymore'

— Yogi Berra

It is said that one of the hardest things in life is
to stop loving a girl who no longer loves you.
I think that stuffing toothpaste back inside the
tube is even harder.

I accidentally said hello to a feminist the other day. My trial begins Monday

Thank you for remaining clam.

I mean, who among us can honestly say they never rode their motorcycle into a brothel asking for coffee?

— C-Milk

I spent a lot of money on booze, birds and fast cars. The rest I just squandered.

— George Best

I started out with nothing, and still have most of it.

I used to go missing a lot...
Miss Canada, Miss United Kingdom, Miss World.

– George Best

I've stopped drinking,
but only while I'm asleep.

I left school in ninth grade to help mother sell
crystal meth. . . good meth though.

I threw a boomerang once
and now live in perpetual fear.

'I was so poor growing up, if I wasn't a boy,
I'd have had nothing to play with.'

– Rodney Dangerfield

I went to see Walt Disney on ice but it's just an old guy in a freezer.

'It's one or two hookers and some blow, I wouldn't necessarily call it partying.'

I always keep a bottle of poison on a kitchen shelf for just such emergencies.

We're not in some dark godless void
on the outer edges of human misery?
No, we're in Nottingham.
Same thing.

- Ade Edmondson to Rik Mayall

'If I still had all the money I've spent on drink over the years, I could spend it on drink'.

- Viv Stanshall as Sir Henry Rawlinson.

'I'm such a good lover because
I practice a lot on my own.'

– Woody Allen

The Irish situation –
they say it's not as bad
as they say it is.

It's better to have loved a short man
than never to have loved a tall.

– Miles Kingston

The weather will be cold;
there are two reasons for this;
one is that the temperature will be lower.

Herr Kutt, German barber.

£50 – how much is that?

What's the French for entrepreneur?

I was caught delicto flamenco.

For all intensive purposes she's illiterate.
The man cannot read or write, he's illiteral.

Two cannibals are eating a clown, one says to the
other, 'Does this taste funny to you?'

I bought a book about a man who was
sent to Alcatraz but got away.
'You're studying the prison system?'
'No, it's just escapism.'

If a man says he will do something, he will do it.
It is not necessary to remind him
every six months.

- Bill Murray

If you kill a killer,
the total number of killers
remains the same.

Dyslexic guy walks into a bra...

'Knock, knock'
'Who's there?'
'To'.
'To, who'?
'Surely you mean to whom?'

'If we don't succeed, we run the risk of failure.'

- Dan Quayle

This is the earliest I've ever been late.

Phil O' Sophy

'Do not be afraid of death
so much as an inadequate life.'

– Bertholt Brecht

Truth left the building a long time ago.

Hell is about seeing the stupid stuff you did.

The dictatorial hunger for power is insatiable.

The cynic: an optimist with experience.

A tragic homage, from one old,
dying white guy,
to another.

This isn't negative thinking, it's positive. You didn't ask to be born, but here you are. Make the most of this flash of lightning in the endless dark. Enjoy yourself. Smoke a cigarette. Eat a fried egg. Jump out of an airplane.

Like all systems the intrinsic contradictions begin to show as fault lines.

Love is not always a bad thing.

Presumed guilty until proven innocent.

A spoonful of nonsense helps the fascism go down.

What is the robbing of a bank compared to
the founding of a bank?'

— Bertolt Brecht

What's the difference if we're looking at an
eternity of complete and utter nothingness and
oblivion?

Where be your gibes now? Your gambols?
Your songs? Your flashes of merriment
that were wont to set the table on a roar?
Prithee, Horatio, tell me one thing.

- W. Shakespeare - Hamlet

Your lifestyle determines your deathstyle.

If it doesn't kill you,
it scars you for life.

Direct democracy is a horrible idea,
just ask Plato.

No matter how long the night,
the day is sure to come.

Certain events can leave you permanently damaged
like a broken plate. You can glue the pieces back
together but it's never exactly the same as it was
before; there are permanent lines of weakness.

It is the sign of an educated mind to be able to
entertain a thought without accepting it.

The clearest mark of intelligence, even genius, is
awareness of one's limits and ignorance.

Criticizing has a brother. His name is Preaching.
They share the same father: Judging.

All comedy is the channeling of a private misery'

– Stanley Baxter,
recounted by Kenneth Williams

All justifications are just a smokescreen
for personal preferences.

A serial killer could have been thinking of
rainbows and unicorns when they
murdered their victims.

If nobody likes your selfie,
what is the value of the self?

Dans toutes les larmess'attarde un espoir.

'Life is full of misery, loneliness, and suffering –
and it's all over much too soon.'

– Woody Allen

Without ugly, there can be no beautiful.

Karma, it's your move.

Iln'y a pas de comique en dehors
de ce qui estproprementhumain.

Life is too short for false friends
and mediocre wine.

Time makes fools of us all in the end.

So Appalling

Putting the dick in dictator.

Time to stop fucking the dog
- I have to get some work done.

Reverse Midas touch.
I think you mean
the Faecal touch.

He shoved his nose up the Flabby Orange Butt,
and enjoyed the toxic aroma.

Semi-solid oral sewage.

Coffee tastes better if the latrines are dug
downstream from an encampment.

I went to see my doctor because I wanted to give up smoking. She said I would have to stop masturbating. I asked why and she said it made it difficult for her to examine me.

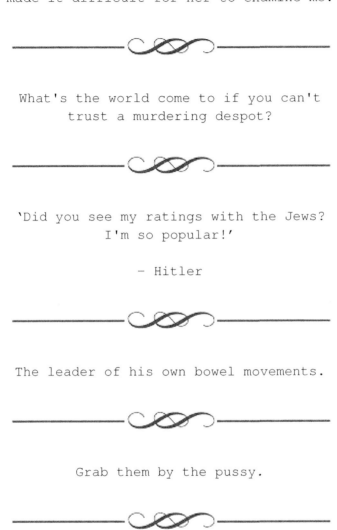

What's the world come to if you can't trust a murdering despot?

'Did you see my ratings with the Jews? I'm so popular!'

– Hitler

The leader of his own bowel movements.

Grab them by the pussy.

Stick your b*llsh!t where it came from.

Cupid stunt

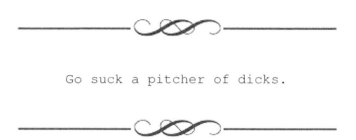

Go suck a pitcher of dicks.

My fist: your vagina.

Here's wishing you a lingering, demoralising death
like cancer, years in and out of hospital, no
breath, rotten teeth, amputations.

Think about it like this, if you get into
trouble as an adult, would you say,
'At least I'm not shitting my pants'?

Everything's a toilet if you're brave enough.

Fuck them and the horse they rode in on.

Q: What are you thinking about?
A: I just hope no one ever finds the body.

I farted.
That's as close as you are
going to get to me giving a shit.

Darling that was not a fart.
I just blew you a kiss from my bottom.

DarkReflections

'What remains of kisses?
Wounds, however, leave scars.'

– Bertolt Brecht

Alcohol, the only thing I like
about being alive.

Of course at this age, halfway to death, a hangover
needs at least three days to bed in.

A dying hope.

I've got a bad feeling about this.

'It always looks darkest
just before it gets totally black.'

- Schulz, creator of Charlie Brown cartoons.

I know what's going on here
but I'm not at liberty to say.

It takes a long time to die of despair.

Talk while you still have a chance.

A mind is a terrible thing to garbage.

Every day I think about his health
- and hope it's getting worse.

Hermann Göring explained how easy it is to
mobilize the public to war: 'The people can
always be brought to the bidding of the leaders.
All you have to do is tell them they are being
attacked and denounce the pacifists for lack of
patriotism and exposing the country to danger.
It works the same way in any country.'

Non-opening parachute for me please.

When you are dead, you do not know you are dead.
It's only painful & difficult for others.
The same applies when you are stupid.

La vie, ça fini toujours mal.

I remember the date exactly, because it was Hitler's
birthday'

- Woody Allen

Chagrin and tonic.

There's a little hint of sweetness,
there's a little hint of death.

I asked my friend in North Korea how things
were going. He said he couldn't complain.

People often act out of misperceptions, anger,
despair, insanity, stubbornness, revenge, pride
and/or dogmatic conviction.

Vodka tastes like regret.

Medicins san morales
- Doctors without morals.

Oddments

PLEASE WEAR A MASK

Foam-flecked rage.

'You're breaking my heart, Jack.'

    - Phillip Marlowe/Raymond chandler,
       In 'The High Window'

Let's just blame china.

Maybe in a vacuum, but not here on earth.

A thundering herd of defenceless souls.

So what you're saying is.

'The dark web ... because it's Black Friday.'

You have unknowingly created a paradoxical
state where the universe cannot resolve and
collapses in on itself due to impossibility and
self-induced instability of space time.

No wonder he's running around, agitated.
The house is infested with bed rats.

These strange days.

I haven't had steak since breakfast.

Want some pork scratchings to go with that?

If we give money to the poor,
they'll only spend it.

And if my grandmother had wheels
she would be a bicycle.

If my aunt had balls, she'd be my uncle.

How's your wife?'
'Compared to what?'

– Henny Youngman

According to a recent survey, English can be fun.

Low rent Fascism

Nothing unites the people of Earth
like a threat from Mars.

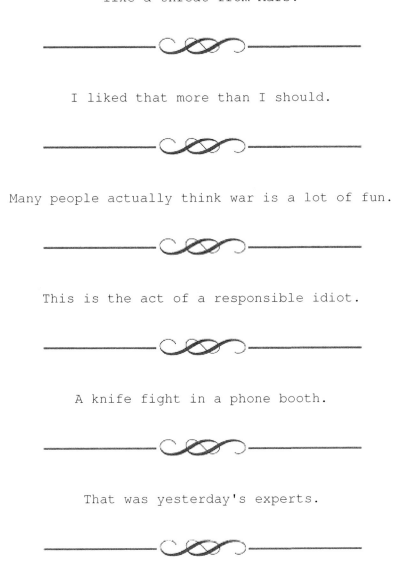

I liked that more than I should.

Many people actually think war is a lot of fun.

This is the act of a responsible idiot.

A knife fight in a phone booth.

That was yesterday's experts.

Definitely a point that should be
discussed with more attention.

The Narcissist's Prayer:

That didn't happen.
And if it did, it wasn't that bad.
And if it was, that's not a big deal.
And if it is, that's not my fault.
And if it was, I didn't mean it.
And if I did...
You deserved it!

I don't know what adverbs, conjunctions,
prepositions, interjections, or past participles
are, but I can still talk pretty goodly.
Or so I've been told…

They cling to guns or religion or antipathy to
people who aren't like them'.

Nothing is ever truly laid to rest in science.

We are grabbers. We are scratchers.

You're looking for something that does not, has not,
will not, might not or must not exist ...
but you're always welcome to search for it.

As any bookmaker or bogus Bhagwant can confirm,
there's always money in selling daydreams to losers.
It's certainly easier than working for a living.

I miss Garrison Keillor.
So does sanity.

'Advertising is the art of convincing
people to spend money they don't have
for something they don't need.'

– Will Rogers

If an anonymous comment goes unread,
is it still irritating?

The stone age didn't end because
there weren't any rocks left.

What is the sound of no hands texting?

Quitting smoking is easy,
I've done it hundreds of times.

Where do we go from here? Mars?

African children could have eaten them fireworks.

I measure my coffee intake in
units of the LD 50.

This is rapidly turning into one
of the worst ideas I have ever had
(there are other strong contenders).

L'alcool tue mais combine sont nés grâce à lui?

'Her smile became a little mechanical'

- PG Wodehouse, The Man Upstairs.

Un égoïste, c'est quelqu'un qui
Ne pensé pas à moi.

Ugliness: the most effective contraceptive.

Confidence is what you have before
you understand the problem.

- Woody Allen

Talent is cheaper than table salt.
- Stephen King

'Give me a small bottle of vodka.
That one, the £4.50. How much is it?'
'Five pounds please mate.'

Switzerland on average is flat.

It's high time we got back to small amounts
of corruption and incompetence
in our political leaders.

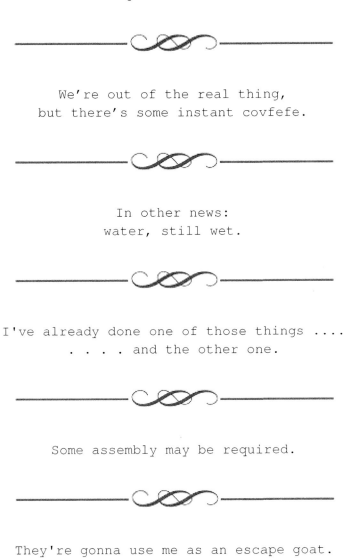

We're out of the real thing,
but there's some instant covfefe.

In other news:
water, still wet.

I've already done one of those things ....
. . . . and the other one.

Some assembly may be required.

They're gonna use me as an escape goat.

Fairy kisses and rainbows.

A gilded celebrity.

Cloudy, with a chance of meatballs.

Beer: not just for breakfast.

Thus Saith the Lord

Drink ye and be drunken and spue
and fall and rise no more.

Jeremiah 25:27

Charm is deceitful and beauty passing.

- Proverbs 31:30

Who can find a virtuous woman?
For her price is far above rubies.

- Proverbs 31:10

God fearing as a New York cockroach

Si vous parlez à Dieu, vous êtes croyant.
S'il vous répond, vous êtes schizophrène.

Fortunately, science, and now the ease by which information travels, mean that there are fewer dark corners where manipulators can get away with the deception which forms the core of religion.

Jésus changeait l'eau en vin. Pas étonnant que douze mecs le suivaient partout.

I went to Lourdes with my wife. No miracle occurred – we returned home together.

'If God exists, I hope he has a good excuse.'

– Woody Allen

'In the beginning, there was nothing. And Godsaid, 'Let there be light.' And there was light. There was still nothing, but you could see it a lot better.'

– Woody Allen

'Faith' is a term with no application for a person
who has a scientific education.

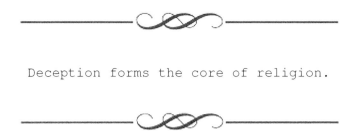

Deception forms the core of religion.

There is no god, just a cold uncaring universe.
We all end up dead and forgotten.

'Religion is the impotence of the human mind to deal
with occurrences it cannot understand.'

– Karl Marx

Talking of Politics

(American)

A US president with no moral authority
flies in to meet a British prime minister
with no authority whatsoever. Each seeking
legitimacy in the presence of the other,
they hail their special relationship like
two bald men might brandish a comb.

The United States of Zimbabwean America

Canada - like America, but better

The land of the thief, the home of the slave.

It's a two-party system, Dumb and Dumber.

Isn't 'Libtard' somewhat derogatory?

It helps, in general, not to be American.

Americans are more importanter than everyone
else.

Rule Britannia

(British Politics)

Sorry, the old Britain can't come to the
phone right now. Why? Because she's dead.

It's every Englishman's right to be
a drunken ignoramus.

It's clear that you have drunk
Jeremy Corbyn's Kool Aid.

Blair stands less chance of being re-elected
than Jimmy Savile's corpse.

If you don't have the cash,
you can always print it.

There will be no way for the next prime
minister or the junior secretary of energy
and climate change,Andrea Leadsom,
to get out of the water dry.

Fear helps advance the conservative argument.

There is of course quite a correlation between
being intelligent and being left-wing,
but that is not causation.

For sale: one Brexit, wheels falling off,
loads of miles on the clock.

The recent suggestions of a
Margaret Thatcher statue
can be best left for the
pigeons to comment on.

If Brexit doesn't happen there
will be blood on the streets.
Blood? Nah, lager maybe.

Another silly EU Parliament decision
that can be given a damn good ignoring.

A scientific approach is advisable; shut one
school and check the results before going
further. May I suggest starting with Eton:
close it permanently.

Rees-Mogg, (British M.P.)
- the idiot's idea of a thinking man.

Peter Hitchens is deeply in love
with a beautiful corpse. (The old UK)

'My honour coloured my judgement'

- Prince Andrew, friend of Jeffrey Epstein.

Thank you for reading my book, I hope you enjoyed it.

Please post a short review on Amazon. Go to
https://www.amazon.co.uk/review/create-review/listing

Your support really does make a difference. I read all the
reviews and value your feedback.

ravelston@seviourbooks.com

The drawings are by Kenny Bamgbose
Kennyvinci1@gmail.com
https://www.fiverr.com/share/7Xv7WL